PUBLISHED *by* PARABLES
Earthly Stories with a Heavenly Meaning

MICROWAVE MADE MAGIC

Stephen Magic Futrell II

PUBLISHED *by* PARABLES
Earthly Stories with a Heavenly Meaning

_____

MICROWAVE MADE MAGIC
Stephen Magic Futrell II

Published By Parables
November, 2019

Printed in the United States of America

Readers should be aware that Internet Web sites offered as citations and/or sources for further information may have been changed or disappeared between the time this was written and the time it is read.

MICROWAVE MADE MAGIC

Stephen Magic Futrell II

PUBLISHED by PARABLES
Earthly Stories with a Heavenly Meaning

My first introduction to cooking in the kitchen, began like most everyone else's. I was brought up to be self-reliant around the house, especially when it came to kitchen activities, and chores. Just knowing how to fend for myself, in and out the house, became my first steps towards independence, and a rite of passage. I believe this was the norm in many homes that resembled my own. We were taught as children early on, how to maintain the home, when left alone. Surely the knowledge of how to cook was essential to it all.

I started off making stuff that required little to no cooking, outside of bowls of cereal, PB&J, or cold cut sandwiches. There really was not much that could be considered cooking. The insertion of the toaster, and "microwave" would change all of the above. At that time I was still only making and heating/re-heating food up that had been previously cooked. Although this ability came in handy before and after school, it was not until my first time over the stove, that I begin to better understand the meaning of cooking. I remember in great detail, my first thing cooked over a hot stove. I was six years of age, and the live-in sitter (by the name of Kim). Decided to aid, and assist me in my capabilities in the kitchen. I truly appreciate 'Kim'. For she passed on the knowledge of how to whip up a simple cheese egg scramble. That in turn would be the thing that sparked my passion for cooking.

I'm also thankful for the cooking instructions I received from my mother, aunt's, and grandmother's. Between that group of extraordinary women, I have learned enough to be considered a very skilled cook/creator in the kitchen. It all started with that first "cheese egg scramble", and it's been on ever since. I never would've imagined that through the act of cooking, a true passion for food, and all things Culinary Arts would develop, and begin to grow. I admit that in the beginning my relationship with food, was one of basic survival. This consisted of eating for the purpose of simple nourishment. But then came the desire to create, learn, and master most of the recipe's I came across. I also developed the habit of frequently tuning in to a few cooking shows. That really allowed me to hone my skills, and extend my limited knowledge. I became familiar with different flavors, food textures, cooking terms, and techniques. All of these things helped me become a skillful cook, with almost no formal training, (with the exception of the aforementioned).

I am currently incarcerated, and in prison cooking can be one of a few things, good, bad, basic, or made by Magic. I'm always thinking of ways to improve a recipe, or even create one. The possibilities are vast, when it comes to food, and cooking. But this can only be said for those who know how to burn (operate the 1 & 2's). To be equipped with only a microwave, hot pot, hot surface, or hot water for cooking methods while in prison. The most average of individual's would surely fail, or fumble, if ever presented with the task of making a meal, at least one worth sharing amongst others. However, prisons throughout the world are where creativity goes to die, or take a hiatus. So when given what the jail, or prison canteen offers up for food selection. Those who are innovative, become creative, and Microwave Magic tends to happen. In this Book I will be presenting a number of different recipes. This will give you more insight into what's on the menu, while on this side of the gate.

Now before I begin the breakdown of each recipe, I have to provide you with the list of allowable ingredients I'm working with. Everything made in here, must be made with purchased commissary. The food selection, and ingredients are slim pickings, (with the exception of third party care packages). Even so, this does little to stop the creativity when cooking. Honestly the lack of ingredients, proves to be part of what keeps me motivated. It challenges me to become a more innovative thinker, and improvise when I do whip. I'm also sure it enhances my cooking skills. If I'm able to get it done without the usual requirements, just imagine my level of creating, adding flavor, and enhancing food recipes with what's called for. I have included a copy of the canteen's food items that are available to give you more of an understanding. Now depending on your positioning at the time of reading this, you may be able to substitute different components. I advise that when you do cook/create, you do so according to your own taste, that's truly what works best.

     I also would like for it to be understood that this is not your traditional cookbook of recipes. You will not be provided with exact measurements, accurate cooking utensils, or even nutritional facts. Your basic needs will only include a few microwave safe bowls, a tumbler cup, and durable plasticware (knife, spork, or spoon). All of the recipes can be made using the aforementioned cooking methods. The instructions may seem a bit complex when explained. But surely, I'm more than capable of simplifying it for you.

I'm also sure that by doing this, it will shine a little light on my own creative/cooking abilities.

Although I'm in here, I try to remain in a creative spirit given my circumstance. So, I have a few signature dishes in the lineup, and some shared/passed on. I've had the opportunity to spread, and break bread with some sharp individuals. It's safe to say, I'm not the originator of all the recipes in the book. But I have made each one, and personally placed my signature on them that's for sure. Cooking in your own style, and according to your taste is pretty universal. I believe that adding your own personal twist to a dish, is part of the artistic side of Culinary. I'm sure everyone is capable of making a bowl of noodles. But only you can whip up a batch to your acquired taste.

I invite you to take each recipe, and re-create it to your own specifications. Or you can choose to follow the leader, its your kitchen. I will leave it up to you, but just be sure to shine whenever you do...then

HAVE AT IT, AND ENJOY!

Canteen Food & Drink Items

Lemonade Mix

Fruit & Grain Bar Strawberry

Granola Bar Chocolate

Lemonade Mix

Tropical Fruit Punch

Cherry Drink Mix

Super C Orange Drink

Red Vines Licorice

Lemonade Candy

Atomic Fire Ball

Wild Fruit (sugar free candy)

Starlight Mints

Sweet & Salty Trail Mix

Sunflower Kernels

Peanuts

Hot Cocoa

Cappuccino

3oz Instant Coffee

8oz Ground Coffee

3oz Instant Coffee

Columbian Blend Coffee (8oz)

Columbian Blend Coffee (16oz)

Decaf Coffee

Coffee Creamer

Powdered Milk

Wyler's Tea with Lemon

Green Tea

Chili w/ Beans

Chorizo Beans

Refried Beans

Black Bean w/ Peppers

Cheddar Cheese Mix

Queso Cotija Grated Cheese

Mozzarella Cheese

Jalapeno Squeeze Cheese

Cream Cheese, plain	White Bread
Wheat Bread	Bagel plain
Cinnamon Raisin Bagel	Hershey's w/ Almonds
Flour Tortilla	3 Musketeers
M&M w/ Peanuts	Ruffles Potato Chips
M&M Plain	Salsitas Chips
Snickers	Nacho Tortilla Chips
Snickers Almonds	Pitted Olives
Milky Way	Stuffed Olives
Reese's Peanut Butter	Tortilla Chips
Payday	Spam
Snickers	Bacon (fully cooked)
Cheese Rice	Pepperoni
White Rice	Buffalo Wing Chips
Fritos Corn Chips	Halal Hot Beef Sausage
Pork Rinds	Beef Summer Sausage
Hot Cheese Crunchies	Spicy Beef Sausage
Tortilla Chips	Microwave Popcorn
Hot Corn Chips	Vanilla Wafers

Chocolate Chip Cookies

Duplex Sandwich Cookies

Lemon Sandwich Cookies

Chocolate Sandwich Cookies

Taco Mix

Roast Beef & Gravy

Beef Stew

Chicken, Chunk white meat

Carnitas De Cerdo (pork)

Smoked Oysters

Jack Mackerel

Hot Sardines

Fish Steak / in green chili

Tuna

Mackerel Fillet

Graham Crackers

Snack Crackers

Saltine Crackers

Whole Wheat Crackers

Chocolate Sandwich Cookies

Matzos

Rolled Oats instant

Berry Colossal Crunch

Toasted Oats Cereal

Honey Nut Cereal

Marshmallow Mateys

Powdered Eggs

Shrimp Cup of Noodles

Chicken Cup of Noodles

Chicken Ramen Soup

Beef Ramen Soup

Hot Vegetable Ramen Soup

Chili Ramen Soup

Honey

Strawberry Jam

Peanut Butter Chunky

Peanut Butter Creamy

Instant Potatoes

Mrs. Dash Seasoning

Vegetable Flakes

Chopped Onions

Cascabella Peppers

Jalapeno Slices

Red & Green Peppers

Hot Garlic Chili Sauce

Salsa Sauce

Sweet & Hot Sauce

Soy Sauce

Pizza Sauce

Barbeque Sauce

Sriracha Sauce

Salsa Verde

Ketchup

Mustard

Mayo

Hot Sauce

Buttermilk Ranch Dressing

Stevia Sweetener

Sugar Individual Packets

Sprinkle Sweetener

Fruit Cup

Lean Meal (meal replacement)

Protein Bar

Topical Island Fruit Snacks

Mixed Fruit Snacks

- ***<u>Big Breakfast Bagel</u>***
- ***<u>Bagel Sandwich (smothered)</u>***
- ***<u>Pin Wheels ---Signature dish</u>***
- ***<u>Cell Sushi---Signature dish</u>***
- ***<u>Egg Rolls---Signature dish</u>***
- ***<u>Heart Attack Wrap---Signature dish</u>***
- ***<u>Stuffed Sausage (seasonal)--- Signature dish</u>***
- ***<u>Burritos</u>***
- ***<u>No Bean Burritos---signature dish</u>***
- ***<u>Pizza</u>***
- ***<u>Pizza Bowl</u>***
- ***<u>Mexican Pizza</u>***
- ***<u>Layered Bowl</u>***
- ***<u>Tortilla Shell Pockets</u>***
- ***<u>Tamales</u>***
- ***<u>Nachos</u>***
- ***<u>Frito Pie</u>***
- ***<u>Chili Cheese Fries---Signature dish</u>***
- ***<u>Fish Cake Patties (over rice)</u>***
- ***<u>Fried Rice</u>***
- ***<u>Fish Dish</u>***
- ***<u>Miracle Meatloaf (Tuna Loaf)</u>***
- ***<u>Sweet & Sour Pork Bowl</u>***
- ***<u>Kung Pow Chicken</u>***
- ***<u>Dim Sum</u>***
- ***<u>Chicken & Dumplings---Signature dish</u>***

- ***<u>Chicken Enchilada Pie</u>***
- ***<u>Chicken Mole</u>***
- ***<u>Chicken Alfredo</u>***
- ***<u>Orange Beef Bowl</u>***

In this line-up of dishes, I've included some of my hardest hitting recipes. I also may have mentioned in the intro, that this is not your traditional cookbook. But to help you better comprehend some of the abbreviated text. I've included this index;

btl = bottle

bg(z) = bag

cup = Cup

pc = Piece

pk = Pack

pkt = Packet

sp = Spoon

spf = Spoonful

slc = Slice

slv = Sleeve

seas. = Seasoning

Stk = Stick

Big Breakfast Bagel (makes 2 sandwiches)

Ingredients:

2 Cinnamon Raisin Bagels

2sl Spam (optional)

1pk Powdered Eggs

2pk Cream Cheese

1pk Fully Cooked Bacon 2pk Jalapeno Slices

Strawberry Jam

I get that some of these components might seem like clashing flavors, but I assure you, they work well together. Try it first, then determine if it's for you, or not.

~Split the bagel and spread the cream cheese on one half, spread the strawberry jam on the opposite half- then set aside-

~In a microwave safe bowl, cook bacon in sealed packet for 1 ½ to 2 minutes. Once cooled, remove from package, place in bowl and allow bacon to sit uncovered (this gives the bacon a crisper texture)-

~Place spam in a bowl and cook for 2 minutes, just enough to heat through- then set aside with the bacon-

~To cook your eggs, pour them into a bowl, add water and stir continuously. Once all the dry mix has been incorporated, season your egg mixture to taste-

~Use a separate bowl for cooking your egg rounds. Pour the egg mix in the bowl to coat the bottom completely, place bowl in the microwave for 1 ½ minutes, or until the egg is cooked through, remove microwave and fold your egg round to fit your bagel bottom-(make desired amount of eggs)-

~Once all the prep cooking is complete, begin the building of your Breakfast Bagels-

~*I.E.*- bottom half of bagel-spam-sliced jalapeno-egg-bacon-top half of bagel-

Re-heat the completed sandwich for 1 ½ to 2 minutes, then... ***Have At It, And Enjoy!***

Bagel Sandwich (Smothered makes 2 servings)

Ingredients:

2 Plain Bagel

Barbeque Sauce

1pk Pepperoni

1pk Chili w/ Beans

1stk Mozzarella Cheese

2pk Jalapeno slices

2pk Jalapeno Squeeze Cheese

1 Spicy Sausage

1pk Roast Beef (w/o gravy)

With this sandwich your work load is in the prep cooking, so set yourself up for success before you begin.

~Cut the sausage into slices, then place sliced sausage, and jalapeno slices in microwave safe bowl, fry them for 1 ½ minutes, remove from microwave and, pour desired amount of barbeque sauce over sausage & peppers and stir. Once ever thing is coated, place in microwave for additional 1 ½ minutes -set aside for sandwich assembly-

~Rinse roast beef free of gravy, then add it to a bowl with chili w/ beans. Stir/mix both together, season to taste, then microwave (covered) for 3 ½ to 4 minutes, remove and let stand (until dish assembly)-

To Assemble

~Split Bagels and apply jalapeno cheese squeeze to each half, layer pepperoni and sausage to a desired number of layers. Place your constructed bagel into microwave safe bowl, and pour over the remaining sauce and peppers-

~Pour roast beef chili over each bagel, dice mozzarella cheese up into cubes, and sprinkle over each bowl evenly-

~Place in microwave for 3 to 4 minutes, remove and add ranch dressing (if desired)-

~Allow bowl to sit for 2 to 3 minutes, then get at that thang with a spoon, then...

Have At It, And Enjoy!

<u>Pin Wheels (makes 3 to 4 wraps)</u>

<u>*Ingredients:*</u>

<u>3 to 4 Flour Tortillas</u>

<u>1pk Fully Cooked Bacon</u>

<u>1pk Jalapeno Slices</u>

<u>4pk Cream Cheese</u>

<u>2pk Jalapeno Squeeze Cheese</u>

This recipe is more of an appetizer than anything else, but you're more than welcome to make it. Then decide how, and when you will serve it. Because this dish is made with tortilla's, you will complete all prep work, then you will begin the assembling of your Pin Wheels

~Fry your bacon to a desired crisp- it's pre cooked so you won't need more than 1 ½ to 2 minutes- then set aside-

~Take your sliced jalapeno and dice into smaller pieces-

~Empty your packets of cream cheese into a bowl, and add your diced jalapenos, mix together well to create a spread-

~Reheat your tortillas in the microwave for 60 seconds, to make them more pliable-

~Apply the spread generously over the tortilla, then add 2-3 strips of crumbled bacon over the cream cheese (evenly), add a squirt of jalapeno squeeze cheese-

~Roll your tortilla up tight, leaving both ends open, then cut your rolled wraps into 1 inch thick Pin Wheels pieces, then...

Have At It, And Enjoy!

Cell Sushi (makes 4 rolls)

Ingredients:

4 Flour Tortillas	*Soy Sauce*
1pk White Rice	*4pk Mayonnaise*
Sriracha Sauce	*2pk Jalapeno Slices*
2oz Vegetable Flakes Squeeze Cheese	*2pk Jalapeno*
2pk Mackerel Fillet	*1pk Smoked Oysters*

This dish was concocted in the cell under a quarantine lock-in. Given the specific set of components, this would be considered an acquired taste. I dubbed it cell sushi, but it's far from raw fish. It can be consumed without any microwave heat.

~Add some veggie flakes and white rice to a bowl, dice your jalapenos up, then add to white rice-

~Add hot water (from coffee maker/hot pot), and allow your rice to soften and swell, drain any remaining water and set aside.-uncovered-

~Open mackerel, and oysters, then drain away all of the oil. Pour into a bowl, and add mayo, squeeze cheese. Mix these ingredients together into a chunky paste-like the consistency (set aside)-

~Squirt the sriracha sauce over the surface of the tortilla, then spread evenly-

~Apply a generous amount of rice to the tortilla, so it's well covered. Place a portion of fish paste down the center of your rice covered wrap-

~Roll the tortilla wrap tight, then slice crosswise into 2 inch pieces. Place in a bowl and dress with soy sauce   , then...

Have At It, And Enjoy!

Egg Rolls (makes 12 to 15)

Ingredients:

1bg Powdered Eggs   Veggie Flakes

2pk Cascabella Peppers

1bg Vanilla Wafers 1pk Stuffed Olive

2pk Mackerel Fillet/or Oysters (for the oil)

1bg White Rice   2 ½oz Chopped Onions

Sweet & Hot Sauce

1bg Peanuts (crushed)

Soy Sauce

Your choice of Meat (sausage, spam, chicken, pepperoni)

This is an absolute signature creation all my own, I have yet to see someone attempt it. The process is a bit tedious, but the end result is well worth the extra effort though. With most every meal, you're going to want to get the prep cooking out the way first, this meal is no different.

~Begin by cutting up your peppers, and meats, pour you rice into a microwave safe bowl-

~Drain the fish oil over the rice, then stir to coat the rice completely. Place the bowl of rice in the microwave, and dry cook for 1 ½ minutes. Remove from microwave and then stir (repeat 1-2x),add some onions, veggie flakes, meats, and peanuts. Then mix thoroughly, and dry cook once more for 1 ½ minutes. Remove from microwave and

then pour soy sauce over combo rice(while still hot). Stir rice then add a small amount of water (just enough to cover the rice)-

~Place bowl in microwave, and cook until done and water is evaporated. Fold in oysters or mackerel, then cover (set aside)-

Egg Roll Wrap

~Crush vanilla wafers into a fine crumb-

~Combine powdered eggs and water to the specifications on the package, then mix with wafer crumbs until you have a loose pancake batter consistency-

~Place enough batter in the bowl to cover the bottom, microwave for 1 ½ minute or until done (you now have an egg roll wrap)-

~Place rice and meat concoction in egg roll wrap, squirt sweet & hot sauce over rice, then roll your egg roll up closing both ends (repeat until all wraps are rolled), then...

HAVE AT IT, AND ENJOY!

Heart Attack (makes 2 servings)

Ingredients:

2 Flour Tortillas

Pizza Sauce

2 Spicy Beef Sausage

2pk Jalapeno Slices

1pk Pepperoni

1pk Pitted Olives

2 Mozzarella Cheese

Queso Cotija Grated Cheese

Now this recipe may sound a little ridiculous to hear, or read out loud. But that's because it is, especially given its title. Regardless of how it may sound, it is as tasty, as it is intensely labeled.

~Split the sausage down the middle lengthwise (don't cut through the back half of sausage)-

~Then cut a slice of mozzarella cheese to the length of the sausage, place mozzarella in the split sausage, chop the rest of the mozzarella into pieces (then set aside)-

~Take your tortilla and spread a nice amount of pizza sauce over the surface, apply chopped pieces of mozzarella on top of sauce, the layer pepperoni over cheese-

~Chop your olives and jalapenos, then spread over the layer of pepperoni. (it's going to resemble a Pizza, but that's another recipe altogether)-

~Once you've completed those steps, place the spicy sausage stuffed with cheese in the center of your tortilla-

~Drizzle pizza sauce over the sausage, and tortilla surface-

~Then roll the tortilla up like you would a burrito (be sure to seal both ends)-

~Place in microwave safe bowl for 6 minutes, remove from microwave and check for doneness. If you're satisfied, let it cool for 2 to 3 minutes.

Otherwise you can heat it up for an additional 2 to 3 minutes. Remember to let it cool, then...

Have At It, And Enjoy!

Stuffed Sausage (seasonal) makes 2 servings

Ingredients:

2 Garlic Seasoned (Christmas Sausage)

2stk Hot Pepper (Christmas Cheese)

1bg Chunk White Chicken

2oz Chopped Onions

3oz Veggie Flakes

2pk Sliced Jalapenos

Now this is a rare classic sure to impress just about anyone its prepared for (with the exception of vegans, vegetarians, and those who don't eat pork products), everyone enjoys this concoction.

~You're going to re-hydrate your chopped onions, and veggie flakes in some hot water, while waiting for them to swell-

~Chop your hot pepper cheese in to small cubed size pieces-

~Cut your jalapeno, then add them to your cheese, combine your chunk white chicken to the mixture, mix together well (then set aside)-

~Split the garlic sausage down the middle lengthwise (butterfly-like), then scoop out the center guts, (creating a cavity-like a boat)-

~Take the guts of the sausage, and cut into pieces, add pieces to your chicken & cheese mixture (this will be your stuffing)-

~Add your re-hydrated vegetables to you filling, and stir well to fully incorporate components-

~Fill each half of the sausage with the stuffing, then close up the sausage, bringing both halves together-

~Wrap in some plastic wrap, then microwave for 6 minutes, remove from microwave, let it cool for 2 to 3 minutes more, then...

Have At It, And Enjoy!

Burritos (made with beans) makes 12 burritos

Ingredients:

1pk Flour Tortillas

1pk Roast Beef & Gravy

1-2pk Chili w/ Beans

6-8 Jalapeno Squeeze Cheese

3oz Chopped Onions

4pk Cascabellas Peppers

1pk Beef seasoning

3-4 Spicy/or Beef Sausage

1pk Chorizo Beans

Black/or Refried Beans

My version of burritos are nothing like most I've seen made in here. I make it a point to pay attention to all details whenever I cook. You can decide to use one kind of dehydrated bean, along with your chili w/ beans, or you can choose to use more than one. I will better explain my method for you though...

~To prep your dehydrated beans, empty beef seasoning, and chopped onions to a bowl, allowing seasoning to dissolve, onions to soften-

~Add your black, or refried beans to your seasoned water, and give, and then time to swell. Stir in your chili w/ beans, and set aside-

~Cut up your sausage, and peppers combine both to the same bowl. Then rinse your roast beef free of gravy, and add to the sausage/ peppers. You will add more seasonings (to taste), and then fry in the microwave 3 to 3 ½ minutes, set aside-

~Empty your Chorizo beans into a bowl and warm up for 2 to 3 minutes, making them easier to work with-

~Heat tortilla up in the package for 90 seconds, then flip them over and heat up for another 60 seconds, (this will make them more pliable when rolling)-

~To build your burrito's, spread chorizo beans over the surface of the tortilla, add your sausage peppers, roast beef mixture. Scoop beans over the top of your meats, squeeze the jalapeno cheese over all of the contents of your built burrito. Roll up your tortilla nice, and tight. After building all of the desired amount of burrito's, reheat when ready to eat, then...

Have At It, And Enjoy!

Burritos (w/o Beans) makes 12 burritos

Ingredient:

1pk Flour Tortillas

3 oz Chopped Onions

2 Spicy Sausage

2bg Roast Beef (w/o gravy)

2pk Peperoni

3pk Cascabella Peppers

1cupCheddar Cheese Mix

2bgz Cheese Rice

4oz Veggie Flakes

Not everyone I have broken bread with, have been fans of all the food available on the commissary. So I came up with this recipe, because not all my comrades eat beans. But everyone who've had them, enjoy these burritos. With all of these recipes, the prep work has to happen, before the cooking can begin.

~Cut up your sausage, peppers, and rinse roast beef free of the gelatinous gravy, (set aside)-

~Empty your cheese rice into a bowl, add some veggie flakes. Pour in hot water, until the rice is covered, and allow to swell up

~In a large bowl add a generous amount of cheddar cheese mix, chopped onions, cascabella peppers, and veggie flakes. Pour in hot water, and stir until all dry ingredients are reconstituted, and well incorporated-

~Continue to stir adding water until your mixture reaches a loose soup-like consistency (like cheddar broccoli soup)-

~In another bowl, shred your roast beef, and mix with your spicy sausage (season lightly). Then fry for 2 ½ to 3 minutes, drain excess grease and then stir into cheese mixture-

~Microwave your cheese rice for 4 to 5 minutes, or until remaining liquid has evaporated, and rice is cooked through-

~Fold cooked rice into cheese sauce mixture(this will create the desired thickness, capable of holding up I a tortilla wrap)-

~In a microwave safe bowl, fry pepperoni for 1 ½ to 2 minutes, remove and drain the grease from meat-

~Warm up your tortilla wraps for 90 second, flip then heat for an additional 60 seconds. Then begin the assembling of your burritos-

~On a tortilla place 3 to 4 pepperoni on the surface, place 3 to 4 scoops of Cheese base mix over the top of your meat. Then roll and fold your burrito wraps up tight-

Before eating, reheat for 2 ½ minutes, then let stand for 1 minute (this will properly meld your flavors), then...

HAVE AT IT, AND ENJOY!

Pizza(makes 1 serving)

Ingredients:

1 Flour Tortillas

Pizza Sauce

½pk Pepperoni

1stk Mozzarella Cheese

1 Spicy Sausage

1pk Jalapeno Slices

1pk Pitted Olives

Queso Cotija Cheese

I know how making a pizza with tortillas may sound, but it's a prison recipe. It's also surprisingly a sure enough substitute for pizza crust. Plus, I got a cooking method that will insure you make it the way it should be made.

~Prep 'Errthang': Cut up your sausage, peppers, slice the olives. Dice or shave your mozzarella as thin as possible, then set aside-

~Place your tortilla on a piece of paper towel, and then microwave on high until tortilla becomes crisp-

~Spread a layer of pizza sauce over the tortilla, then begin to build your pizza-

~I.e. Cheese- Pepperoni- Sausage- Olives (optional)- Jalapenos-

~Once you've built your pizza, microwave for 1 ½ to 2 minutes, then sprinkle with queso cotija cheese, then...

Have At It, And Enjoy!

Pizza Bowl (makes 1 serving)

Ingredients:

Pizza Sauce

1pk Jalapeno Slices

1 Bagel

2pk Mayonnaise

1stk Mozzarella Cheese

1bg Buffalo Wing Chips

1pk Jalapeno Squeeze Cheese

Queso Cotija Cheese

1 Sausage

1pk Ranch Dressing

½pk Pepperoni

This is one of the few recipes, that's a hand-me down. So I give credit to the contributor, thanks. You're very appreciated-

~Crush buffalo wing chips, then add minimal water, mash the moist chips together-

~Then begin by creating layers with the potatoes-pepperoni-sausage-mozzarella-jalapenos-and pizza sauce (you should be able to build 2 to 3 layers until complete)-

~Break the bagel into pieces in a bowl, add 2 packs of mayonnaise to bagel pieces. Place the lid on the bowl, and shake. Then add queso cotija grated cheese, and shake once more-

~Put the bagel pieces on top of the layered bowl as a topping, then squeeze jalapeno cheese over the top of bagel pieces-

~Cook in microwave for 3 to 3 ½ minutes, remove and add ranch dressing, then...

Have At It, And Enjoy!

Mexican Pizza (makes 1 pizza)

Ingredients:

2 Flour Tortillas

1stk Mozzarella Cheese

Salsa Sauce

1pk Jalapeno Slices

1pk Cascabella Peppers

2pk Jalapeno Squeeze Cheese

1bg Chorizo Beans

2spf Hot Garlic Sauce

1pk Pepperoni

1 Chili Soup (seasoning)

Mrs. Dash Seasoning

1 Spicy Sausage

I got this recipe idea from a yearning for fast food. The process to make it is similar to the one for making a Pizza (with the exception of a step or two), but let me explain.

~With all my recipes, you have to get your prep work out the way first. This will make the entire meal simple to create-

~Cut your sausage into cubed chunks, then slice the peppers, and dice up your mozzarella (set aside)-

In a bowl dissolve the chili seasoning packet, add chopped onions and allow to swell, stir in chorizo beans and season with Mrs. Dash, and hot garlic sauce (to taste) incorporate all ingredients well-

~Microwave beans for 3 to 4 minutes, remove microwave and let stand-

This recipe calls for two tortillas per Mexican Pizza, so be precise when prepping

~Place tortillas on a paper towel and heat until firm, and crisp (repeat until you have two tortilla per pizzas)-

~Once you've completed frying the shells, you can begin the process of building your Mexican Pizza-

~On the bottom tortilla spread a thick even layer of bean mixture-

~Place top tortilla over beans, then spread a layer of salsa sauce over the top tortilla-

~Sprinkle mozzarella cheese over salsa, then add sausage, pepperoni, and peppers-

~Squeeze Jalapeno cheese over the top, and reheat for 1 ½ to 2 minutes, then...

Have At It, And Enjoy!

Layered Bowl (makes 1 serving)

Ingredients:

3-4 Flour Tortillas

1pk Pepperoni

1 Spicy Sausage

1bg Chili w/ Beans

2pk Jalapeno Slices

2oz Chopped Onions

Hot Garlic Sauce

½cup Cheddar Cheese Mix

(jalapeno squeeze, or mozzarella will sub)

This dish is an attempt to be more creative with the ingredient's for burritos. Its's also very versatile, and can be made with a verity of components, it's up to you in how choose to proceed.

~Prep your components, by slicing your jalapenos, cut sausage into bite size pieces, dice up your mozzarella (optional). And whip up your cheddar cheese mix-

~Rehydrate your opinions in warm water, then add your chili w/ beans (season to taste) and add hot garlic sauce. Microwave for 3 minutes and then set aside-

~Fry sliced sausage for 2 minutes and then set aside-

~Heat up 2 to 3 tortillas for 30 seconds each-

~Place 1 tortilla in a bowl, press down, and around the side, and bottom-

~Place a layer of sliced sausage over tort, top with cubed mozzarella cheese-

~Pour Chili w/ Beans over sausage and cheese-

~Top Chili/w Beans with a layer of pepperoni, then add a layer of jalapeno slices-

~Spoon cheddar cheese mix, or squeeze cheese over the layer of jalapenos-

~Squirt sriracha across the top layer created, and then place a tortilla atop your first layer-

~Then repeat the layer building process from the first step using your remaining ingredients. You should have about 2 or 3 layers when finished-

~Place bowl in microwave for 3 ½ to for 4 minutes, remove and allow to cool, then...
Have At It, And Enjoy!

Tortilla Shell Pockets (makes 12 servings)

Ingredients:

Meat of choice (2 sausages , 2 chicken, or 2 pepperoni)

Cheese of choice (2^{skt} Mozzarella, 4 Jalapeno Squeeze, or 1cup Cheddar Cheese mix)

Pizza or Barbeque sauce

Seasoning of choice (Mrs. Dash, Classico, Seasoning packet)

This recipe is very flexible and left up to your own specifications, I'm just giving you the technique. I received this recipe from a buddy of mine, and this is how he simplified it.

~Slice and dice meats to small portions-

~Prepare cheese (if using powder), or dice into small pieces-

~Chop peppers-~Cook meat to desired texture, and drain any grease, lightly season meat-

~Heat tortilla until pliable-

~Imagine a small square in the center of the tortilla, place sauce or cheese within the center (3 or more inches)-

~After the sauce , or cheese, add your selection of meat. Then top with peppers, and add more cheese (remember to keep the layers even). You will then fold one side over the other leaving he meat and cheese in the middle. Next you will fold one end over towards the center-

~Flip the tortilla over and fold the other end towards the center, this will secure the filling inside, creating a square pocket-

~Grill one side until brown (on the surface of the coffee maker). Flip and repeat on the other side then let cool-

~If reheating in the microwave, use a bowl (left uncovered), heat for 60 to 1 ½ minutes, then...

Have At It, And Enjoy!

<u>Tamales (makes 16 servings)</u>

<u>*Ingredients:*</u>

<u>*1bg Tortilla Chips*</u>

<u>*2Salsa Verde (for green)*</u>

<u>*2pk Meat (roast beef*</u>

<u>*no/ gravy- carnitas de cerdo)*</u>

<u>*4oz Chopped Onions*</u>

<u>*1btl Hot Garlic, or ¼btl Sriracha sauce*</u>

<u>*(for red)*</u>

<u>*1 Chicken seasoning packet*</u>

This recipe can be tedious, and cause the average person to duck the whole process. But once you do it, it's nothing to it.

~ Crush your tortilla chips into a fine powder, or crumb -set aside-

~Empty your choice of meat into a bowl, and rinse well-

~Add enough hot garlic, sriracha, or salsa Verde to coat the neat well, add chopped onions. Then Microwave for 8 10 minutes, allow to sit-

~In a tumbler empty the contents of chicken seasoning packet, then pour hot water in the cup, filling it up to the rim. Stir to dissolve-

~In a big bowl, pour broth over crushed chips, mixing well to create a ball of masa dough-

~Once dough is at the right consistency, you be able to portion out palm size balls-

~Take dough balls, place in between plastic wrap, and on a clean flat surface. Begin to flatten dough in to a round shape-

~Add a spoon full of meat filling, and fold up all side of masa dough to close, and form tamale, wrap in plastic, and set aside-

~In a hobby box place a small amount of water in the bottom. Then place a Styrofoam meal tray in hobby box , on top of the water. Place tamales on top Styrofoam try, and place in the microwave for 6 to 8 minutes-

~Repeat until all tamales have been steamed in the hobby box, once complete...then

Have At It, And Enjoy!

<u>Nachos (makes 2 servings)</u>

<u>*Ingredients:*</u>

<u>*1bg Tortilla /or*</u>

<u>*Nacho Cheese Chips*</u>

<u>*2pk Jalapeno Slices*</u>

<u>*1bg Black /or Refried Beans*</u>

<u>*2oz Chopped Onions*</u>

<u>*1 Spicy Sausage*</u>

<u>*1pk Pitted Olives*</u>

<u>*Mrs. Dash*</u>

<u>*1bg Roast Beef w/o Gravy*</u>

<u>*Classico Seasoning*</u>

<u>*1cup Cheddar Cheese Mix*</u>

<u>*Salsa Sauce*</u>

<u>*1 Chili Soup (seasoning packet)*</u>

I'm sure see all of the ingredients on this list seem like a lot of components. But not all of these items are necessary to make a Nacho round. I add everything so that my flavor profile is "Official-Official"-

~Cut up your sausage , chop your peppers (set aside). Rinse the roast beef , and shred with knife, or spoon, season with Mrs. Dash- chopped onions- and classico seasoning (to taste). Microwave on high for 3 minutes (set aside covered)-

~Add chopped jalapeno to your sausage and fry in the microwave for 2 to 2 ½ minutes (set aside)-

~Add the chili soup seasoning packet to some hot water first, season with chopped onions, Mrs. Dash, and classico seasoning (to taste). Then combine your black /or refried beans with seasoned hot water, and allow to marinate and swell. (this method will give your beans much more flavor)-

~After your dehydrated beans have been reconstituted, stir in chili w/ beans, place in microwave and cook for 3 ½ minutes, (set aside until it's time to dress your Nachos)-

~In a tumbler cup whip your cheddar cheese mix to a desired consistency. Then add shredded roast beef and stir, microwave for 1 ½ minutes (set aside), drain any remaining grease from sausage and peppers-

~Slice pitted olives, and set them aside. they will be used as a topping-

~To Build your Nachos, add a layer of chips to a bowl and cover with a layer of beans. Pour cheese mix over the beans, top cheese with sausage & peppers. Squeeze salsa sauce over sausage & peppers, top with slice olives. Repeat the process to create layers, or eat the first serving, saving the fixings for later (I layer my nachos though until all chips are covered, then reheat for 2 minutes)then...

Have at it, And Enjoy!

Frito Pie (makes 2 servings)

Ingredients:

1½ Fritos /or Hot Corn Chips

2^{stk} Mozzarella Cheese

1 Spicy Sausage

4pk Jalapeno Squeeze Cheese

2bg Chili w/ Beans

2pk Jalapeno Peppers

1pk Chorizo Beans

3oz Chopped Onions

1pk Pepperoni

Mrs. Dash, Classico Seasoning (optional)

This is a rendition of a meal introduce to me by my mother. Her version was dubbed "Haystacks", and had the addition of fresh vegetables. Made due with what I had at my disposal.

~Cut up sausage, and peppers then fry for 1 ½ minutes-

~Set a cup of Fritos/corn chips aside until the assembling of the pie. Crush the remaining chip into a fine crumb, add hot water (until chips become a masa like dough)-

~Season beans, and mix well, then microwave for 3 minutes-

~Chop mozzarella in to cubes, and set aside until the assembling-

~In a bowl add chorizo beans, your seasoning, and a little water, then microwave for 3 minutes or more, (you want your beans to be thick, but spreadable)-

~Once all components are prepped, you can begin the assembly of your Frito pie-

~Take the masa like dough and press it around the circumference of the bowl like a pie crust-

~Pour your chorizo beans in the chip mold and spread across the bottom, and along the sides-

~Sprinkle a portion of whole chips over the bottom of mold-

~Top the chips with cubed mozzarella, and cover with Chili w/ Beans-

~Layer beans with sausage, more chips, mozzarella and Chili w/ Beans (building layers within the bowl)-

~Cover the top with pepperoni, jalapeno squeeze cheese, and jalapenos peppers-

~Microwave on high for 5 minutes (allowing flavors to meld together), let stand for 2 minutes, then...

Have at It, And Enjoy!

Chili Cheese Fries (makes 1 serving)

Ingredients:

1bg Chili w/ Beans

1cup Cheddar Cheese Mix

1 Spicy Sausage

1pk Jalapeno Slices

1bg Ruffles /or Buffalo Wing Potato Chips

This definitely one of those dishes that requires some creative thinking, and an even more creative cooking method. But it slaps once you figure it out, Trust That!

~Crush potato chip down to crumbs, and add just enough water to moisten the chip crumbs. Form chips into a dough like consistency-

~Flatten dough to within an inch thick, and then cut into desired fry shape, and length. Cook in the microwave until crispy, place in a separate bowl (and set aside covered)-

~Cut sausage and fry in microwave for 1 ½ to 2 minutes, and set aside-

~Pour your chili w/ beans in a bowl and microwave for 2 to 3 minutes (season to taste)-

~Whip your cheddar cheese to desired thickness, and add chopped jalapeno slices-

~Pour your chili w/ beans over your fried French fries, top your chili w/ beans with your sausage, and pour over cheese mix (reheat for 1 ½ to 2 minutes), as always...then

Have At It, And Enjoy!

Fish Cake Patties over rice (makes 2 servings)

Ingredients:

2bgz Jack Mackerel

2pk Smoked Oysters

Sweet & Hot Sauce

4oz Veggie Flakes

Hot Garlic Sauce

1 ½slv Saltine Crackers Soy Sauce

2bgz White or Cheese Rice   Mrs. Dash

2 Beef or Spicy Sausage 2 ½oz Chopped Onions

Growing up in my household, this was a meal known as Salmon Croquette. But even then, it was made with Mackerel. It was a favorite amongst many, none the less though.

Fish Cakes

~Clean and rinse your mackerel, then add your oysters, season with hot garlic and Mrs. Dash-

~Crush saltines into a fine crumb and add to your fish. Mix with your jack mackerel/oyster combo until incorporated well-

~Form in to palm size patties, and fry individually for 2 to 2 ½ minutes or until cooked through. When all patties are complete set aside (covered)-

Rice

~Add rice, veggie flakes, and chopped onions to a bowl, then pour water over rice until fully covered, and allow to swell-

~Cut sausage into slices, then add them, and jalapeno slices to a bowl and fry for 2 minutes-

~Place rice in the microwave and cook to reduce the remaining liquid. Top with sausage & peppers-

~Place the desired number of fish cakes over your rice-

~Mix sweet & hot sauce with about a spoon full of hot -garlic sauce, and drizzle over the top of each patty-

~Microwave on high for 1 ½ to 2 minutes to reheat the dish, then...

Have At It, And Enjoy!

Fried Rice (makes 1 serving)

Ingredients:

1bg White Rice

1 Spicy Sausage

1pk Cascabella Peppers

1oz Veggie Flakes

Soy Sauce

2oz Chopped Onions

¼bg Stuffed Olives

1pk Mackerel Fillet (essential for oil)

1sl Spam (optional)

The method for frying rice can ruin a bowl, and the dish if you are not cautious. But when it's done right it's its own reward.

~Pour desired amount of rice into a microwave safe bowl, add the oil from the mackerel. Then stir to coat all of your rice evenly as possible, fry rice in microwave for 1 minute. Remove from microwave and stir to distribute heat in bowl evenly. (Repeat this process until rice become lightly darker in color)-

~Remove your rice from the microwave, and while its still sizzling hot, pour soy sauce over, and stir (this will add both seasoning, and moisture)-

~Chop your sausage, and spam up into small chunks. Dice your cascabella peppers into pieces, and stir into your rice-

~Sprinkle in veggie flakes, and chopped onions, add a minimal amount of water (just enough to cover the rice)-

~Then fry in microwave on high for 3 minutes, or until the water has reduced completely. Once done, stir rice once more before serving, then...

Have At It, And Enjoy!

Fish Dish (makes 1 serving)

Ingredients:

1bg Jack Mackerel

1oz Chopped Onions

1pk Oysters

2oz Veggie Flakes

1 Spicy Sausage

2pk Jalapeno Squeeze Cheese

1bg White or Cheese Rice

1bg Peanuts (optional)

1pk Cascabella Peppers

Your choice of Sauce (sweet & hot-BBQ- hot garlic)

Your Choice of seasonings (Mrs. Dash-salt & pepper- soup seasoning packet)

I know the number of components seems like a lot. But I feel its only worth your time. If this dish is prepared correctly.

~You're going to rinse and clean your jack mackerel thoroughly (remove all brine, and bones)-

~Place cleaned fish in a bowl and then season with sauce, Mrs. Dash, and seasoning packet (to taste). Cover with a little water, microwave with lid partially on for 5 to 6 minutes to boil and reduce the liquid-

~Cut sausage into slices, and dice peppers, then fry in the microwave for 1 ½ to 2 minutes. Drain oil from sausage, and stir in oysters (set aside)-

~Place rice in a bowl, add veggie flakes, and chopped onions then cover rice with water. Microwave until rice soften, cooked through, and water has been reduced completely-

~Cover rice with cooked fish and drizzle with your choice of sauce-

~Top fish with fried sausage and peppers, add oysters, then top with peanuts. Squeeze jalapeno cheese over the top, once all components are combined reheat for 2 ½ minutes...then

Have At It, And Enjoy!

Miracle Meatloaf (Tuna) makes 1 serving

Ingredients:

2pk Tuna

2oz Chopped Onions

1 ½slv Snack Crackers

Mrs. Dash

Barbeque Sauce

2oz Powdered Eggs

This is a hand me down recipe given to me by a creative individual. I appreciate him for sharing his method with me, for that I added his dish to the lineup.

~Place 1 lean meal scoop of powdered eggs in a bowl, add seasoning, and onions, with about ¾ scoop of water. Stir together until there are no lumps in eggs (a smooth consistency)-

~Add Tuna and crushed crackers to the bowl, mix until well incorporated-

~Add barbeque sauce and , Mrs. Dash (about 2 spoonful's), mix all ingredients until smooth and consistent. (make sure that you have a bowl with a lid that can cooked on)-

~Use a spork to press down the tuna mix into the bowl, try to remove all air pockets that may form. Press until you have a shape, that is the same circumference of the bowl all the way around-

~Use a fork to poke air hole into your loaf mold, place bowl in a leveled microwave and cook for 6 minutes.

~After 6 minutes remove loaf from microwave, and place lid on the bowl, do a steady, quick flip. (if done correctly, the loaf will drop down as one piece, unto the lid) -be sure to cover lid with plastic-

~Place the loaf back into the microwave, and cook for 2 minutes, remove loaf and let stand for a minute or two, until slightly cooled-

~Add barbeque sauce like you would place icing on a cake, (do not use too much, you don't want to overwhelm the loaf with sauce)-

~Place back in the microwave for 2 to 3 minutes, or until barbeque sauce has darkened-

~Remove from microwave, let stand to cool, then...

Have At It, And Enjoy!

Sweet & Sour Pork Dish (makes 2 to servings)

Ingredients:

2 Spicy Sausage

3pk Jalapenos Slices

1bg Hot Pork Rinds

3oz Veggie Flakes

1bg Carnitas De Cerdo

4oz Red & Green Peppers

2bgz Cheese Rice

Sweet & Hot Sauce

This is definitely a signature dish, and a real fan favorite every time it's made.

~Slice your sausage, place in a bowl, and add diced jalapeno slices-

~Rinse Carnitas De Cerdo, and add to the bowl of sausage & peppers, add generous amount of sweet & hot sauce. Place in the microwave and fry for 5 to 6 minutes, remove the stir to coat the meat evenly. (set aside)-

~Place rice in a bowl, add veggie flakes, and then cover with water. Cook rice in microwave for 4 minutes, or until water is completely reduced, cover rice and set aside-

~Rehydrate sweet red & green peppers until softened, and dry pork rinds and stir to fully incorporate the two. Combine this mixture with sausage, carnitas, and jalapenos. Add a touch of sweet & hot sauce, and stir once more until all are well coated-

~ Evenly top your cooked rice with the meat and pepper combo. Reheat in the microwave altogether for 2 to 3 minutes, then...

Have At It, And Enjoy!

Kung Pow Chicken (makes 2 servings)

Ingredients:

1bg Chunk White Chicken

1pc Chow Hall Chicken

1 spf Chunky Peanut Butter

2sp Hot Garlic Sauce

1bg White Rice

2oz Veggie Flakes

1/2bg Peanuts (crushed)

Mrs. Dash or Chicken seasoning

You can also substitute plain noodles for rice with this dish, either way it full of flavor. It's also not something you get every day.

~Strip your chow hall chicken from the bone, and shred, then place in a bowl and add chunk with chicken. Season your chicken, and reheat in the microwave for 2 minutes, (set aside)-

~In a separate bowl add 1 to 2 healthy spoonful of peanut butter, pour a little water over (to soften).

Then add hot garlic sauce to your peanut butter (to taste), stir together, mixing well to create the kung pow sauce-

~Place sauce in the microwave and heat for 2 minutes to heat it through, remember to add a little water as need it, (you want a pourable sauce-like consistency)-

~Add you reheated chicken to the kung pow sauce and incorporate both well, then set aside-

~In a bowl add rice, and veggie flakes, then cook rice for 4 minutes reducing all remaining liquid, or to a desired texture-

~Top rice with Kung Pow Chicken sauce, reheat in the microwave for 2 minutes, let stand for 1 minute. then...

Have At It, And Enjoy!

Dim Sum (Stuffed Dumpling)makes 2 servings

Ingredients:

1pc Chow Hall Chicken (chicken from the chow hall menu)

½ cup Creamer (plain)

2bgz Chunk White Chicken

1 ½oz Veggie Flakes

4 Flour Tortillas

2oz Green & Red Peppers

1cup Cheddar Cheese Mix

3pk Jalapeno Peppers

1oz Chopped Onions

2bgz Cheese Rice

1bg Salsa Verde

My inspiration for this dish was heavily influenced by an Asian classic. That's the reason I paid homage in the dishes label.

~Take your piece of chow hall chicken de-bone, and shred it to bite size chunks. Combine that chicken with the chunk white chicken, and season to taste-

~Then add your salsa Verde, (this will be the filling for your dumplings). Place in the microwave and cook for 3 to 3 ½ minutes, then set aside-

~To make dumplings, take and shred your tortilla into strips, place in a big bowl, add just enough water to moisten the tortilla strips, then knead them together to create a dough-

~Tear of palm size portion of the dough, and roll them into balls, then flatten each ball in to a round shape-

~Once you've achieved the desired size, and shape you begin filling each one with 1 to 2 spoonful of your chicken mixture (depending on the size of your dough round). Mold the dough into a ball around the chicken, creating a cavity, then roll between your hands to smooth their surface. Once all dumplings have been formed, set a side-

~In a big bowl for cooking, add your cheddar cheese mix (about a cup) creamer (½ cup), veggie flakes, red & green peppers, chopped onions, and diced jalapenos. Then pour in water and stir until all ingredients have been incorporated, and you have a soup-like consistency-

~Submerge your dumplings in the soup mixture (adding more water as needed), and microwave for 6 minutes. Remove from microwave and agitate. Then place back in the microwave for an additional 6 minutes, remove and let stand-

~Cook rice to desired texture, then top with your dumplings (3 to 4). Pour soup mixture over the top of the stuffed dumplings and rice, then...

Have At It, And Enjoy!

Chicken & Dumplings (makes 2 servings)

Ingredients

2pc Chow Hall Chicken

2oz Red & Green Peppers

2bgz Chunk White Chicken

2pk Cascabella Peppers

5 to 6 Flour Tortillas

2 oz Chopped Onions

½ Cheddar Cheese Mix

1bg Cheese Rice

1 ½oz Veggie Flakes

3 Chicken Soup seas pkt

I know it may deem like I just gave you this recipe, although similar to the previous dish. Some of the techniques are different, let me run it down for you though.

~Strip and shred the meat from the bones of your chow hall chicken, and combine with chunk white chicken. Then season taste, and add your chopped cascabella peppers-

~Microwave on high for4 minutes, when don set aside-

~Shred your tortilla into small pieces and place in a big enough bowl for mixing. Pour water over tortilla pieces, and allow them to absorb the liquid for 1 to minutes-

~The tortilla will take on a very soft dough like texture (and that's the consistency you want)-

~Began portioning the dough into small balls, and then roll between hand to form tight pieces of dough. Place all formed dough pieces in a bowl, and then set aside-

~In a big bowl (hobby box), add your seasoning packets, red & green peppers, chopped onions, and veggie flakes. Then pour hot water over all ingredients, and allow them to soften, and your seasoning to dissolve. (this will create a broth)-

~Bring broth to a rolling boil in the microwave (this will require a few couple of cycles)-

~Then remove from microwave and place your seasoned cooked chicken, allow the broth to come back up to a rolling boil (another cycle or two)-

~Then add all of your rolled dumplings and cook for 2 cycles of 6 minutes apiece. Once this is done, remove all dumplings, and add a ½ cup of your cheddar cheese mix and stir thoroughly. Then and dumplings back to the mix and reheat for 5 minutes, remove from microwave and let stand-

~Cook your cheese rice to a desired texture, once done, top with dumpling and spoon over chicken cheese soup mixture and serve, then...

Have At It, And Enjoy!

Green Chili Chicken Enchilada Pie (*makes 1 serving*)

Ingredients:

3 Flour Tortillas

2 Spicy or Beef Summer Sausage

2pk Chunk White Chicken

1bg Salsa Verde

1stk Mozzarella Cheese

2pk Cascabella Peppers

3spf Hot Garlic Sauce

~Prep your cheese, peppers, and sausages, by cutting them into small pieces-

~Empty your chicken into bowl, and add dehydrated onions, stir and mix well (season to taste)-

~Combine cheese, sausage, and peppers into bowl with chicken, and onions. Place in microwave for 3 minutes set aside-

~Place your tortillas in the microwave for 90 seconds to soften, and make more pliable, then fill up each tortilla with an even helping, and roll them up. (you should have 3 per bowl)-

~Combine salsa Verde, with a few spoons of hot garlic sauce, then pour over rolled tortilla (covering completely)-

~Microwave on high for 4 ½ minutes, then remove and allow to cool for a minute, once cooled, then...

Have At It, And Enjoy!

Chicken Mole (makes 1 serving)

Ingredients:

1 Chunk White Chicken

10z Veggie Flakes

1pc Chow Hall Chicken

1spf Peanut Butter (chunky)

1/2bg White Rice

1spf Hot Garlic Sauce

1/4cup Hot Cocoa (powder)

1pk Jalapeno Slices

These may seem like unusual components, but I assure you, they come together, if done properly.

~Strip, and shred your chow hall chicken from the bone, and combine it with your chunk white chicken meat, set aside-

~In a separate bowl add ¼ cup of cocoa powder, then add just enough water to moisten powder turning it into a paste, stir in a spoonful of hot garlic sauce, add more water (enough to cover) then add a healthy spoonful of chunky peanut butter-

~Place bowl in microwave, and cook for 2 ½ minutes to meld flavors, and more water to loosen up the sauce-

~Take your stripped chicken and season to taste, then microwave on high for 2 minutes-

~Once you've reheated your chicken, add to your mole sauce, stir and then cover. Let stand while you prepare your rice-

~Pour desired amount of rice into a bowl into a bowl, then add your jalapenos, and veggie flakes. Place rice in the microwave and cook until the desired texture is reached-

~Top rice with Chicken Mole' mixture, and reheat if necessary, once the dish has been reheated, then...

Have At It, And Enjoy!

Chicken Alfredo (makes 1 serving)

Ingredients:

2pk Chunk White Chicken

Red & Green Peppers

1 ½cup Cheddar Cheese Mix

Veggie Flakes

1cup Creamer (plain)

1stk Mozzarella Cheese

Chopped Onions

2pkRamen Noodles

Hot Garlic Sauce

Mrs. Dash

This dish is another set of tedious tasks to complete, but it's up there with one of the best I've come up with.

~In a big enough bowl for mixing, add your red & green peppers, veggie flakes, chopped onions, and 1 cup of creamer-

~Pour hot water over dry ingredients to dissolve creamer, and reconstitute vegetables (this mixture will begin to look like a cream chowder)-

~Once all ingredients are dissolved, and rehydrated, stir in 1 ½ cup of cheddar cheese mix, continue to stir (adding water when mixture begins to thicken). Once everything is well mixed set aside-

~Take your bowl of chicken and add Mrs. Dash, and hot garlic sauce to taste, then microwave for 2 minutes-

~Remove chicken from microwave and stir into alfredo cheese sauce, and set aside-

~To prepare your ramen bring a bowl of water to a rolling boil, then remove from microwave, add two ramen to the boiling water. Place bowl bake in the microwave, and allow to come to a rolling boil. Let it cook for 2 minutes, then remove and drain free of all water. (You want your noodles to be cook, and free of any liquid - al dente'-)-

~Cut your mozzarella in to small cubes and toss in you cooked noodles, (save ¼ cup of mozzarella for topping the dish)-

~Place your alfredo in the microwave and heat it through for up to 5 minutes, remove from microwave and pour over your noodles, and toss together, then...

Have At It, And Enjoy!

Orange Beef Bowl (makes 2 servings)

Ingredients:

2bgz Roast Beef & Gravy

½cup Lemonade Mix

4-6oz The Juice Of 2-3 Oranges

The peel of 2-3 Oranges

3 Beef Soup seasoning pkt(s)

2bgz White Rice or Ramen

3oz Veggie Flakes

This dish was once easier to make , when tang/orange drink was available on the canteen. Since it's been removed, I have and to improvise, and make adjustment. But it still comes together.

~In a bowl empty your beef seasoning, then add hot water to dissolve, and stir in ½ cup of lemonade mix-

~Add the juice of oranges to the mixture, then cut the orange peels into strips, and place in the broth-

~Empty roast beef & gravy into the flavored broth, stir well, and allow it to marinate over night-

~After you allow it to marinate, place in the microwave on high for 12 to 15 minutes (about 3 or more cycles), set aside-

~Add veggie flakes to noodles, or rice, and cook through to an al dente texture-

~Drain beef broth from roast beef, and orange peels, then dress them over you noodles or rice (which ever you choose), then...

Have At It, And Enjoy!

As long as I can remember, I've always had an interest in cooking. I enjoy the creativity that it requires. So it was only natural for me to take the food items available to me, come up with a way to enhance them. If I was ever asked why I put this book together, I'd admit that I needed an outlet to express myself creatively, and nothing comes more natural to me than cooking. But it's actually more to it than those facts. In truth I became skilled in the act of cooking in a microwave while living a life where I regularly cooked, and served up a different concoction. It had absolutely nothing to do with food. But through this felonious endeavor, I was definitely eating. Placing my knowledge of how to cook, along with my understanding of service, gave me all the skill required to be a good cook. Once I had a changing of my mind to reposition my aim. I then began to apply my talents towards something more positive, Cooking. This trip to prison gave me a direction to head towards. Becoming a certified Chef is my destination, and owning/running my own restaurant is my goal.

Allow me to fill you in, through my own skills, and experience. Also I would just like it to be known that this book was created in prison. Where the use of any type of camera, for the sake of photographing these dishes, was very much prohibited.

So although there are no pictures to illustrate the dishes. The instructions are a simple step by step that anyone can fallow to achieve a complete recipe. I've also enjoyed writing my version of a cookbook, and sharing a piece of my mind with you. So I'm working on something else that segues into some more of that. My next project will be my own story. It's sure to grasp anyone who takes the time to read it. My Life's A Movie!

Acknowledgements

I enjoyed putting this project together, and I had some help along the way. For that I must express my appreciation, and thanks. To all the females in my life, who made sure I knew my way around the kitchen (mother, grandmother, aunts, sister, and Kim). To the RN (Ms. B), for all her help with the attempt at illustrating the project (it proved to harder than I thought). Thanks to my un-official editor (Sam M.), for combing through the work for me. To the buddy of mine (Travis B.), who shared two of his own recipes with me. To the close female friend of mines at DW (Merita C.S.), who also shared her version of a recipe. Thanks a tone to all who provided aid, and assistance through the creating this cookbook. My deepest appreciation to my older cousins (Mr. & Mrs. D. Butler), for supporting me and my vision. Through their efforts, this book was made possible. I'd also like to like to issue much thanks to my publishing team, for all the work dedicated to my first literary project.

About the Author

Stephen Futrell is a proud father of three. He is born, raised, and harvested in the city of Denver, Colorado. A skilled cook, who aspires to become a certified chef once fully liberated. He's also got other literary projects in the works, so be on the lookout.

To contact write to:

Stephen Futrell #128943

P.O Box 392004

Denver, Co. 80239

About the Book

    This book is full of creative expression, and innovative creation through food, in an unfamiliar form. Each dish is what's considered good food while in prison. I stand by each one, and can win over anyone with the way I prepare them. This is my attempt to simplify the cooking process, for people who find themselves in a similar predicament. Or, it's for the people who live far outside an environment like prison, with an inquiring mind about the food available while inside. But absolutely no need, or desire to visit the confines of a jail first hand. You will find answers to the most frequently asked questions, pertaining to what's on the menu.

MICROWAVE MADE MAGIC

MICROWAVE MADE MAGIC
Stephen Magic Futrell II

MICROWAVE MADE MAGIC
Stephen Magic Futrell II